Every.

Every.

Alexia Zakariya

Seed Royale Publishing

CONTENTS

DEDICATION vi

One | Introductory   1

Two | HAIR.   3

Three | MEDICAL.   8

Four | F*CK IT.   13

Five | HERB.   19

Six | RELIGION.   23

Seven | PRIDE.   28

Eight | COUNSEL.   32

Nine | DARKNESS.   36

Ten | LIGHT.   40

Eleven | VENTING.   43

OUTRO   47
ABOUT THE AUTHOR   53

I Dedicate this book to my Husband Alonzo Gross and our 3 babies: Beya, Myka & Zowiee. I wouldn't be here without any of you. You all are that driving force forward for me. My hardest days I get through with your unconditional love.

I love you.

Copyright © 2021 by Alexia Zakariya

All rights reserved. No part of this book may be reproduced in any manner whatsoever without written permission except in the case of brief quotations embodied in critical articles and reviews.

First Printing, 2021

One

Introductory

Call It an Intrusive thought, call it an Omen. (Man I'm blunt...Ima tell it like it is). I'm not going to edit myself it's just coming out raw how I receive the thoughts. The name of this book actually was chanted at me while I was Unconscious. Being that I was admitted in the Mental hospital, considering the vibe is basically a Prison Cell without the locked doors, I felt my soul freeze and could not really write (we got no privacy to do so anyways they read your personal thoughts in there)...anyhow, So I got back to graffiti, and I would code the fuck outta that shit.

I Make up a language they don't understand. One thing about survivin',though, after awhile it ain't really livin'. When U feel as though you have to backspace every moment and encounter in your life. That's how it feels being a Woman of Color in the US of A. (I Hate this Country—Constantly a thought in my brain) But anyways...back 2 what I was sayin'.

The Idea of Every—At first I'm like What the fuck did I just experience (I cuss a lot just a heads up I'm writin' unscripted)...I was in there and they weren't really carin' 4 me as a person, as a P.O.C, or as a woman. I was havin' bad side effects from their meds, and I lost consciousness a couple of times. I woke up in cold sweats shakin'. IT 'TWAS a supernatural experience which has happened to me several times in there (I Spent a portion of my 20's in and out). This specific time was different, I heard Ancestors Chant EVERY so I drew some graffiti. But I'm like what was that? Why was that the word I heard right when I woke up. I literally just connected the dots today while I was in pain again (something about being in pain makes U hear on a different wave if U feel what I'm sayin'). I think it was GOD, Ima leave it at that.

I have a lot of Inner thoughts, many ideas, my 1st 2 books were Poetry I'm thinkin' something different with this one. Ima see where my pen leads me. Ima Start out talkin' 'bout thoughts chapter it out on that concept coupled with other shit. Enjoy. I keep my Intros Rather ShorT...2 SHORT (Ha...Shoutout lol I'm a young Oldhead my Kids Love 2 Short).

Two

HAIR.

Don't Touch MY Hair....I just...Wanna "FEEL THE TEXTURE" ...NA CHILL...I'm not UR pet, I'm not UR... (gettin' HEATED this is my INNER THOUGHTS, I GUESS They're intrusive) UGH...I'm welcoming my thoughts at this point in my life and Ima be straight up, I don't believe in Intrusive thoughts!!! I think they are necessary thoughts. They let U know how UR heart is feelin' at the moment of what you're feelin'. Like when people wanna touch your damn hair or tell u to 2 "tame" UR hair for their comfort. Fuck that. Fire me then Ima wear my natural KINK. Call me what U WANT. Don't hire me then. U know how many hours it takes me 2 straighten it?? My "ITALIAN" Mother had it in my head 2 always straighten that shit when I went to jobs, when I went 2 interviews. Man she must of been so ashamed of my DAD's DNA. Every interview thinkin' are they goin' 2 say something? Is it white girl lookin' enough 4 them? Email back read: We have found someone else better suited in their wording, that is my wording. Basically they sayin' fuck off you don't fit my company image. This is why I started this book about hair....

I'm at the point in my life where I'm just embracing my NATURAL HAIR. I used to cut it, I used to put chemicals in it, I used 2 used 2...all for their "COMFORT"....FUCK THEIR COMFORT.

I'm not here 2 bring comfort and PEACE. I'm actually here to make them UNCOMFORTABLE...

Let me tell U ABOUT WHAT my MIXTURE means 2 me....It means an Inner War. It starts with my HAIR. I have about 3 different textures goin' on. I have Curly, Wavy, and THICK puffy hair. The hair transitions into the SOUL. U feel me?

The hair transitions 2 who I am. I am very PROUD but I am also very INSECURE. How U C me is UNIMPORTANT 2 who I AM. U notice the CAPS and also the lowercase? (My INSECURITIES). This is how I feel always havin' 2 whitewash and edit myself in this society that we live in.

I grew up with an extremely racist ITALIAN Woman. She got with my Dad he is Afro-Egyptian/Palestinian. They are very proud people. Straight up from Egypt/Palestine. She raised me to purposely feel disconnected from my own people. Hence the name "Alexia". Alexander the Great oppressed many...I hate my name but I've grown 2 love it in a way because it explains my history but honestly the name brings me pain. My existence brought my Mother pain. My hair to her was a "Sore" reminder.

As much as she tried to "Beauty Pageant me up" & Straighten my black hair, make me into this pristine version of herself (not myself) the worse she became, while trying to bring me down with her. Keep in mind this is the same woman that insulted my whole fuckin' being, so I have no love or respect 4 her. Now before U go throwin' bible scriptures SHE AIN'T A BIBLICAL TYPE MOTHER...She the type of Mother that wanna C ME DECEASED...SHE THE TYPE OF MOTHER THAT WANNA C ME UNDER 10

FEET....So get that through CHURCH PEOPLES (Anyway let me take another puffa REEFER)...

...(Much Betta)...Excuse my PTSD...Hair is so personal 2 me. As it probably is to U if you're still readin'. Whoever put it down it wasn't meant 4 them. Ima keep that in there cuz I'm tired of being edited as U probably are as well. Which is why I'm goin' Natural with my hair. My homegirl hooked me up with some nice braids. There's something about seein' your homegirl from back in the day and her doin' your hair and talkin' to u as your sista that heals ur inner pride...I'm tellin' U at this point in my life I struggle with PRIDE...

Hair though....That's the 1st thing Women go 2 when we're hurtin'. We either cut it all off 2 cleanse our brokenness or do it differently. I'm tellin' U that whole hospitalization prison shit I went through where my hair was constantly matted every day cuz they didn't provide U with SHIT 2 do your hair in there with (U HAD TO GET CREATIVE, amidst a pandemic especially). When that shit was braided, I felt my MARRIAGE HEALIN'. I'm in a vulnerable state of being that's why I HATE MUHFUGGAS touchin' my damn hair. I hate that Hair is such a CONDEMNATION TO ANYONE THAT AIN'T WHITE. I SAID WHAT I SAID!! It's HAIR ENVY they feel ...the reason Y they want us "TAMED"....Anyways, Anyways, rest assured if you're offended this book is not 4 u so just stop readin' now. Trust & Believe I cannot just walk away when I feel what I feel I have 2 endure it. We either react or don't react. I'm reactin' from a writer standpoint after silently protestin' 4 weeks while I was in the hospital by not speaking.

I'll explain...It instilled in me a level of anger not havin' nothing 2 do my hair with except 4 this cheap ass white woman comb. Literally...I got mad as PHUCK. Every day they forced us 2 be in group (IF we don't attend these stupid ass repetitive ass groups they basically admit u longer or say you are not complyin' with treatment or whatever they fuckin' say) but I was pissed off because it took me about 2 hours with this dumbass comb 2 even get my hair halfway decent. They already label me a fuckin' threat the moment I walk in, least U could let me do is do my damn hair and look decent. Na...So I protested. 2 Women in there blessed me with braids. Man that was the only way U can get through. It seems so SIMP but I promise U IT IS NOT...It is whitewashing. Even the groups are. U need some kind of BREATHIN' & RETREAT...

I'm out NOW...BUT I'm TELLIN' U...If U have any ounce of KINK in your MAINE...can you understand as to why I started with HAIR? I even started with that over religion....That's how Sacred this subject matter is and that's why it is constantly attacked by WHITE AMERIKKKA. The sad part is the self HATE u FEEL after it is instilled in U over the years. That shit does not fade easily. It is a journey most def. When you start to appreciate your hair, it is normally after u done fucked it up! LOL. My hair's on the recovery but TBH I still don't know how to do braids, I still don't know how to maintain my own hair, my edges or anything. All I know is what I know. All I know is my insecurity over the years. My instilled self hatred by my own BIO MOTHER. I'm sure some can relate. Probably many feel me on that. Embrace that shit. Don't let no one touch it if it makes u UNCOMFORTABLE. 4 the OPEN MINDED ONES THAT ARE PAINED BY THIS...Listen...U need 2 know how we feel thank U 4 still readin'. I wanna bring Healin' 2 many by these words. These are HONEST THOUGHTS UNSCRIPTED. I want to keep SAYING THAT. Keep in MIND...WE HAVE 2 think about EVERY.

(Every. Single. Day. We. Out. Who's. Going. 2. Touch. Our. Hair. Microaggressions. Racism. Predjudice. That. Is. Our. Reality. I'm. Starting. With. Hair. EVERY.)

Three

MEDICAL.

I Don't really trust Medical Doctors. I have my reserves. I've had so many touches with death and side effects over the years the shit that has happened to me still effects me to this day. Let me talk about my MENTAL HEALTH. Just the term in itself sounds a bit ENSLAVED don't U think? Mental= CRAZY & mix together HEALTH to disguise it as CONCERN. That is exactly the masked vibes they put off when U go in there...

Back in the day...when free slaves tried 2 escape sometimes they were stuck in the MENTAL HOSPITAL....THE ONES AROUND HERE...people have jumped out of the windows...The state hospital was featured in "GLASS" then later torn down. Every time I passed that building it brought me terror although I was never there it's like U could feel the SCREAMS...but anyways...

How are we supposed to trust these "Medical Professionals"? Because we are taught 2? Or "It's the right thing 2 do?"...Man listen, I wish MAN did listen and MAN tends 2 Err...This is why I am HESITANT but I'd rather have a DOCTOR that admits that they are INSECURE and not ALL KNOWING then one that claims that I'm INCOMPETENT because I AM ADVOCATING 4 myself...This is MEDICAL ARROGANCE...My EXACT ISSUE WITH DOCTORS...let me explain a little more though because it is a bit deeper than that maybe U can relate or not but let me get the shit out...

Honestly, stayin' on the mental note...I had an extremely terrible upbringing...my BIOMO (That's what I'ma call my biological mother I'm not going to list her name b/c she is not worthy of gettin' a shoutout) was very "Mentally Ill" as they would call it but I call it "Mentally Unstable" because it seemed as though it was mostly directed towards me...Any WHO...She kept tryin' 2 force diagnoses on me and force me in and out of these LOVELY "Mental Encampment Prison HospitalZ"...It worked 4 awhile but as of LATE I've been really ADVOCATING....

THIS is so important and part of the reason "EVERY." was even a CONCEPT...Think about the word for a minute and how it relates to UR MENTAL. I'm sayin' U matter...The Doctors are sayin' MENTAL ILLNESS=CRAZY DISEASE. That is what U mean to them. That is what BIOMO saw as well...think about it. Think about OUR hesitation for "MEDICAL PROFESSIONALS"...

I AIN'T BIPOLAR...I AIN'T SCHIZO...I AIN'T MANIC...I AIN'T SCARED NO MO...

AIN'T MY TIME SO THIS AIN'T A CHALLENGE...but I BEEN THERE BE4...

SO THIS IS 4 those who are mistrusting...

U HAVE A REASON 2 FEEL THIS WAY...U ARE HEARD & LOVED...

I Don't know about these PSYCH meds man…

I am not feelin' these new age tactics to enslave…

Some are OK…
BUT THIS HERB…
THIS PRAYER…
THIS LOW DOSE OF HALDOL (EH//FORCED —It'Z not PRaisE))…
IT ^^ Ain't the worst but something that effects my ability to be MOTIVATED…
That's some CRAZY shit…
I only TRUST ONE Psychiatrist I've had for almost 10 yearZ…
She is HONEST, REAL…
FIND u a HER (SHe is a LATINA—)
Trust me…It mAtters 4 the reasonZ I stated…
THe most frustrating part of getting medical care is getting medical care from someone with WHITE PRIVILEGE…
I will walk the fuck out and never come back.
BUT SOMETIMES…I cannot do that.
Such as these "MENTAL PRISONS"…
When U are given no choice but to have to listen to these doctors,
Forcefully be strapped 2 a bed and stripped with UR COOCHIE showing in restraints…
OR
IN RESTRAINTS IN SOLITUDE
OR
DOWN 2 the DIRTY GROUND WITH A NEEDLE IN U
4 SPEAKING TRUTH…
I'm tellin U that MEDICINE DIDN'T seem GOOD
Either KIlls U, is OK with u 4 the MOMENT…

Or U THROW IT OUT when no one is lookin'
cuZ best believe they KNOW WHAT THEY DO.
THEY MAKE $600 a day off U...
They ain't all bad.
BUt they ain't all good.
They kill Ur soul.
Traumatize U a bit.
Then send U back home.
4 Your Family 2 Deal with it.
U end up Back...
IN & OUT...
Up & DOWN...
INCARCERATION...
This is why I don't like "Medical Professionals"...

On a lighter note.
I once wanted to be a Medical Professional.
Until all of this malpractice.
Until this lack of $ to pursue that dream.
Until I noticed in school it was more about Math & Science.
The teacher said to leave Vo-Tech if we felt like that was a problem.
(I Struggled with both).
I never was Unintelligent. Just distracted.
I learn in patterns & much differently.
SO let's say there is GOOD MEDICINE.
BUT mistrust is REAL (towards doctors)...
All of this is very true and real...

EVERY.

(EVERY. VOICE. SHOULD. COUNT. WHEN. IT. COMES. 2. UR. TREATMENT. PLAN. ADVOCATE. 4. URSELF. BUT. BE. SMART. ABOUT. IT. UNDERSTAND. INNERSTAND. UR. ROLE. IN. THEIR. JOURNAL. U. DESERVE. COMPENSATION. U. ARE. NOT. MENTALLY. ILL. HEAL. UR. MENTAL. IT. WILL. BRING. U. PEACE. U. DESERVE. PEACE. AFTER. PEACE. AFTER. WILL. HEAL. UR. MENTAL. GET. OUT. OF. UR. OWN. WAY. HUMILITY. COUPLED. WITH. PRIDE. ARROGANCE. AT. TIMES. BE. FREE. BE. YE. EVERY.)

Four

F*CK IT.

F*CK IT...2 this PAIN I feel each & every day..

I try to laugh it off, I try to do anything to get it off of me.
It lays Heavy on my CHEST...
I have a heart for people, Man.
I remember the day that I left the hospital,
It was bittersweet. (This last time)...
This brotha was cryin' & screamin' & reached for me. (4 comfort)
I don't know what specifically made him reach out (that happens to me a lot in there)
But it bothered me the pain I saw...
(I said F*ck it to the food and did not eat)

I said F*ck it when I saw Adam get tackled to the ground in there by security.
I don't get how they expect everyone to just sit in their room and relax.
"Just chill out while we kill people in the hallway"
F*ck that. I went out there...
No phone 2 record.
No phone 2 record.
No phone 2 record.

F*ck it, I'm not afraid of death.
I know they could have turned around and murdered me.
Something about how I yelled snapped them out of their trance.
They left low grade threats.
Boxers mixed in with my clothes (that weren't there and weren't mine)
& then they all came up 2 try to forcefully DOPE me up...
Was it a med I was supposed to take? I'm unsure.
I bled for 6 days afterwards they didn't know quite why.
Adam had Epilepsy and it wasn't cool.
I didn't want another brotha dead...
(They extended my stay, triggered me day in and out, the trauma from bearin' witness and also being on the receiving end of forcefully being injected...let me go on...)

There's something about an anger that u cannot put a name behind...
When I was put in restraints, for peaceful assembly
Over medical care that I did not agree with.
Dope veinZ, staff tried to break my armZ,
As spiritual as I felt I felt lifeless...
I SLEPT for 2 straight dayZ
Didn't EAT, SHIT, PEE, SHOWER...
(I was a couple months pregnant with my daughter)
I couldn't say F*ck IT, so I got up & fought back...
In my Heart I said F*Ck it, In my Mind I said "FIGHT BACK"...

I can't force lines that don't flow out of me from time to time.
I have to step away and say Fuck it.
I can't edit out the U.
U caused this Amerikkka.

I have to say Fuck it from time 2 time.
Or I will lose my Mind.
MENTAL health right?
Mental HEALTH right?
I'm white 2 u?
I'm white 2 u?
Yes, U, I'm talking 2?
Did U Hear Rashida Tlaib?
U understand our history better than we do.
There is no way I will allow u
2 WHITEWASH a WHOLE HISTORY...
I put down AFRICAN AMERICAN.
I said FUCK it. UR classification on race is INCORRECT.
U Know This.
It's By Design.
I'm Smoking & Saying
FUCK it.
AMERIKKKA has already made me age twice as fast.
Pac said it best. I couldn't accept simplicity.
U have to say Fuck it in Amerikkka.
F***K censorship.
uc CenSORship.

How do U feel reading this as a Christian?
How do U feel reading this as a Muslim?
How do U feel reading this as an Atheist?

Sometimes I swear I Feel like all 3.
God=Allah but at times who is God right?
Should I say Fuck it?
Or Should I believe?

I say it makes more sense 2 believe.
I know my Soul has already decided.
Don't let pain strip u bare.
Don't lose your soul is tatted on me.

I used to write to Wilson Pickett,
I used to belt to Etta James.
I used to practice to Alicia Keys.
I used to cry to 2Pac.
I used to LOGIC to Common.
Then I said Fuck it.
I'm not tryna lose my life.
I died a total of at least 1 time.
Hereafter is a better term to me.
I came back in Pain.
I said Fuck it.
Lost my memory.
Lost my drive.
Missed Death.
But missed out on life.

Cut out the Liquor. (It burned my chest)
JazZ black & milds didn't make me dance (The cancer paper was in there)
Hookah felt high but left me low & without a voice.
I said fuck it.
I said fuck it.

I walked away from terrible situations harmed.
I walked away from terrible situations scathed.

EVERY.

I am scorned at times.
I have to say fuck it.
It's my therapy.
It's situational.
It's how to fight racism.
U have to have a level of IDGAF.
I can't walk, talk,and cry.
I am not tryna walk, talk, and die.

If it sounds Bitter Blue.
Cool.
I'm listening to Emotional by Carl Thomas.
It's harder than u think to get this out.
From years of sayin' fuck it.
Now I say ENOUGH on the MEDS.
But it's the WEED that is holding my hand.
MY CHEST is burning in AGONY.
DMX just died.
All BLACK MEN DYING at the hands of the POLICE.
I've hurt my black king's heart.
Pride. & scorn.
This is my apology.
I'm tryna let my wallZ down 2 him.
In all wayZ.
I don't post about it.
I don't post about it.
Gil Scott-Heron.
This is how I react 2 Fuck it.
This is what Fuck it means 2 me.
What does it mean 2 u?
What track gets u able to survive fuck it?

It can be a slow death.
I'm not tryna say fuck life.
I'm sayin' Pour out a lil' LiquoR...

(This. Was. A. LONGER. Chapter. How. can. I. explain. How. many. Things. I've. seen. And. experienced. In. 28. Almost. 29. Years. Of. life. In. June. I can't. Neither. can . U. most. Likely. But. just. Know. that. U. have. To. be. Hard. to. the . unmasked. Eye. u. R. whether. that . is. Ur . callousness. Of. soul. Whether. U. mend. Ur. heart. In. private. Only. God. knowZ. Yes. &. No. Self. Is. Coming. Back. IN. u. Have. learned. How. 2. Cope. u. C. black. U. black. Out. or. U. block. Out. in. search. Of. a. Better. Day. live. 4. Today. Pour. out. Some. It's. Tough. Out. here. My. Soul. cried. Out. every. At. my. Moment of Fuck. It. I. felt. Suicidal. If. I. would. Have. said. That. I. felt. They. would. Have. killed. Me. my. Soul. fought. Back. &. The. ancestors. Chanted. EVERY.!)

Five

HERB.

I used to be SOBER minded…kind of.

I would drink 40s, Smoke Hookah, JazZ Black & Mild's…Anything to sort of NUMB myself.

I wouldn't do this all the time.

This is how I coped with my Mental.

This is how I coped with my Lack Of.

Lack of Love, Lack of Support, Lack of Bread, Growlin' Stomach from Lack of Nourishment.

Herb is different.

Herb is Freeing.

Herb numbs but allows U 2 Feel…

I used 2 be against it.

Mainly because I was ignorant, White Amerikkka tries to push this concept into Ur head as well…

That U sit there like a Vegetable.

That ain't the case. First OFF…I just cleaned the whole house.

I cannot do that on Meds, I cannot do that with Liquor (I pass out).

Herb helps me focus, helps me F*cK.

(Not that I have a problem in that area)

It just sort of clears my mind.

I have SOOO much PTSD…

U ever have that Jumpy feelin' in UR soul?

There's something about being oppressed for so long since CONCEPTION that makes U wanna just feel 1. No one quite Understands ur sorrow or ur life story but something about when U take a PUFF Problems also start with the same letter and they somehow PASS. Ain't it ironic that U PASS THE DUTCHIE ON THE LEFT HAND SIDE…

I just…always struggled with so much internally. I spent so many years in solitude. When I met my King, he felt that. We did it 2gether. I tried it maybe once before him, wasn't feelin' it really. I don't know what my disconnect was. Maybe it wasn't a disconnect at all but I felt really attuned. I would spend about 6 hours at least a day singing, lay on a hard wood floor and write. I would stare at the fan. I really LOVED solitude. I really loved my MENTAL.

So many have come and broken my HEART. I act TF and black TF out once this happens. I wish I had smoked back then ctfuuu. But it just was meant to be something I do with my King. It healed something deeper within us that we didn't even know was wrong. We both been through it. We both struggled with the same things.

I like it now, I'm hyperfocused a bit anxious, I get mellow and chill like I used to feel. There's something about PTSD after going through so much in one lifetime that U really wanna tell the trauma C U next LIFETIME, bump some ERYKAH BADU, TEENA MARIE, RICK JAMES, OTIS REDDING, ETTA JAMES, PAC, BIG, ANITA BAKER...PUFF away & Cough & manage 2 also sing. Hey, BeatZ doing Hookah. I stopped that once my voice started going. I need something to cope man this life is 2 hard. God gave us Herb Y not enjoy. Ms. Herb is my assistant. She takes over when I cannot bare this life. It sounds a bit sad, but I am not a happy smoker. There's a part of me that misses me. The MELLOW YEARS. GANJA is what I like now. I feel my soul Come back 2 Me. It's 2 Numb. It's 2 Numb. It's way 2 Numb. Trauma. Trauma. Trauma. Every. (Time I PUff).

(Smoke. That. Sh*T. The. HIGH. EASES. U. WEED. CHRONICLES. ATTUNED. 2. WHAT. U. USED. 2. BE. &. ALSO. 2. WHAT. U. ARE. BECOMING. IT. ISN'T. SO. BAD. IS. IT.? CONGENITAL. HEART. FAILURE. IS. A. MUCH. WORSE. FATE. DR. GANJA. GAVE. ME. THE. PERFECT. DOSE. IF. I. SOUND. LIKE. A. FIEND. SO. I. FEEL. RE-

LIEVED. I. FEEL. GRATEFUL. 2. HAVE. SOMETHING. THAT. DOESN'T. CAUSE. ME. 2. CRY. NONSTOP. EVERY. DAY. &. EVERY. NIGHT. I. LOST. 3. KIDS. WITH. MY. HUSBAND. MAN. SO. MUCH. HAS. HAPPENED. I'M. LAUGHING. AGAIN. CRACKIN'. JOKES. CASUAL. SENSUAL. THAT. BE. ME. EVERY. PERSON. DOESN'T. EXPERIENCE. THIS. POC. PAIN. POC. SORROW. WE. JUST. SURVIVED. PRESIDENTIAL. WHIPLASH. 4. FUCKIN'. YEARS. OF. THIS. ORANGE. MOTHAFUCKIN". MAN. BACKWARDS. ASS. WORLD. U. R. NOT. WHAT. THEY. SAY. AS. MJ. SAID. U. R. NOT. ALONE. EVERY! (Chant that sh*T....+++)

Six

RELIGION.

DEAR DIARY, turned 2 DEAR GOD:

Which turned 2 Jesus, which turned 2 Allah, which turned back 2 God. Which turned Atheist 4 a bit. Which questioned. Which Prophet…Which crossed Ova…Which Lost Consciousness…Which eva since has been connected & disconnected.

"U C WAT U C
IT MIGHT BE HARD
2 BELIEVE…
U MIGHT HAVE 2
PAY A FEE…
2 B FREE>>)((*("…

My Original SELF creeped on back…this was a Poem I wrote when I was about 5 years OLD.

I believed in MONSTERS. IMA keep it real I felt bad Spirits in my house with my BIOMO. I tried to Run away. I packed my stuffed animals and I WAS OUT (Metaphysically speakin' of course).

I always felt a PRESENCE. When I was younger I was TERRIFIED. I didn't like to sleep in the bed by myself. BACK THEN my BIOMO was my MOM and she was good 2 me. She was understanding of my FEAR. Her MAN not so much...A for effort on her part she tried everything to get me to sleep by myself. I just would C figures, I would C Supernatural THANGS...kinda hard to sleep by URSELF without getting terrified...

Back 2 RELIGION...It was neva forced on me. I don't know if it's worse growin' up in a atheist house or a believin' house. My experience was an ATHEIST house. My Dad's Side Super Religious but more so SPIRITUAL.

I always knew I believed in SOMETHING. That was my basic BELIEF...

I relied on that "Something" and later that became "Someone" (Hence, Dear Diary...)

I was ALONE a lot. Sometimes purposely, other times not. I just neva fit in. That's what happens sometimes when U are MIXED. U don't tend to fit in any which way.

THE LONELINESS brought on my CREATIVITY, I Meditated with Candles, With Incense, I was a WORKAHOLIC with a Sex addiction (Stemmed from my multiple rapes) but I still believed in something I was searching 4 something (or someone). It didn't make sense but it does.

I turned to the church. My love & pain comes from the CHURCH. Judgment is healthy but pointin' fingers brings judgment back. I FELL in love with JESUS 1st getting terrified. I HEARD GOD talk 2 ME differently...I was nicknamed DAUGHTER ONE (I Hated my name & didn't know my identity, I felt abandoned by both of my parents). God told me to read Parrables (I spelled it wrong which told me I was in Communion with something higher than myself).

I felt the path I was on was right at the time, my SOUL felt differently and my SOUL also felt very aligned. I WAS PAINED. I noticed. I felt. I cried. I sobbed. I couldn't stop crying and sobbing. What and Y caused this HEARTACHE? I mean at the time I went through a bad breakup but at the same time I WAS OVA THAT...

GOD CAUSED me 2 CRY...I DESERVED 2 CRY...CUZ I WAS NO GOOD...That's how I felt at the church. Every. Single. Church. That. I. Went. 2.

I was homeless at the time. I met my now King. I ran from him. Almost lost him for good. When I started "Seeking God" or so Christianity teaches U....(I always was of God==I didn't need 2 be "Converted")...My SOUL found this lesson out the hard way...

I GOT INTO A RELIGIOUS OBSESSION...I read the bible and I WOULD NEVA ADD UP ANY WHICH WAY I LOOKED. PANIC STARTED, STRESS BEGAN. BEFORE THAN I WAS UNAWARE OF MY PAIN...It was always there...

In this vulnerable state...I almost lost my LIFE...I faced my DEATH. I was kidnapped. I caused my kidnapper 2 CRY & bring me back...IT was a SET UP. No one Cared or really even knew about my disappearance. Some wondered where I was & called but I felt this desire 2 fight. I'm not going to get into what I saw because something about being attacked like that U JUST WANNA BE A BIT SILENT. BUT NOT SILENCED. Although, for years I WAS SI-

LENCED. I've been 2 the MOUNTAINTOP. That was not my HEART'S DESIRE but I pulled through (KIND OF...) It's been almost 10 years, I still feel the effects from that.

It broke my SOUL, It hurt my JOURNEY but it STRENGTHENED ME cuz I SURVIVED. I had an OUT OF BODY EXPERIENCE. MY body was passed out in the car, MY SOUL WAS FIGHTING. SO SO MUCH HAPPENED...I'm finally completely back...

I will never be the same from that experience however...

I hate organized religion.

I've read the bible.

I ordered the QURAN.

I heard PROPHET ELIJAH MOHAMMAD in a vulnerable state.
I still believe in ONE. One is what I believe. I believe in ONE, THREE, NUMBERS. 7 LEVELS OF HEAVEN...ALL OF THAT. God told me 2 Go by my HEART.

My HEART IS WHAT I GO BY. " WHO DO U BELIEVE IN? —TUPAC"...DEAR GOD 3.0— THE ROOTS. MOMENT OF TRUTH—GANGSTARR, (My Darker side) DAMIEN—DMX (Rest Easy) CLIMBIN' THE STAIRWAY 2 HEAVEN WHILST SITTIN' ON THE DOCK OF THE BAY....(O'JAYS & OTIS REDDING)

(EVERY. TIME. I. CLOSE. MY. EYES. AND. OPEN. THEM. BACK. AGAIN. FEELING. A. TOUCH. OF. DEATH. AND. LIFE. AT. THE. SAME. BREATH. I. AM. REMINDED. HOW. FRAGILE. LIFE. IS. AND. HOW. INTERTWINED. IT. IS. WITH. DEATH. WITH. ONE. WITH. THREE. WITH. ONE. I. HEARD. HOW. MUCH. I. ALSO. HEARD. HOW. LITTLE. WE. ARE. VALUED. I. DON'T. KNOW. WHAT. IZ. TRUE. ALL. I. KNOW. IS. FUTILE. THAT. IZ. WHAT. POWERS. C. &. PREACH. ALL. I. KNOW. IZ. WHAT. CAN. B. PASSED. ON. FROM. ME. 2. U. FROM. NEW. 2. RENEWED. FROM. PREACHER. 2. PROPHET. 2. LEST. U. VIBE. WITH. AFTER. EARTH. U. WOULD. NOT. GRASP. THESE. LINEZ. KEEP. UP. NO. MATTER. HOW. UR. VIEWED. DOES. UR. SOUL. FEEL. PEACE. OR. DURESS.??? EVERY.!!! (ChanT)

Seven

PRIDE.

Pride is how you view it.

When U are brought up with a bunch of loud mouthed mothafuckin' people then you learn to have a level of pride.

When U try to love and this PRIDE comes OUT, well then it either pushes U to be vulnerable or it leaves u alone with PRIDE. I was the second person for many many years. I thought I COULD DO BAD ALL BY MYSELF. IN fact, many women think this HENCE THAT BEING ONE OF MY FAVORITE TYLER PERRY MOVIES...

The thing is can we really?
The thing is does Pride serve a purpose?
Is it useful for men to meet women with PRIDE issues?
With their GUARD UP?
I'll Say Yes, U can say NO...

I'm not tryna be easy to LOVE.
I've been easy to HATE.
My MOUTH can get real FOUL...
But...I can also get real SWEET...
UNDERNEATH if u grasp what I'm sayin...

We live in a Society where we cannot be SOFT.

We are sexualized at a YOUNG AGE as soon as we get an ASS or TITTIES or our COOCHIE lips get FATTER...

Hence PORNOGRAPHY, HENCE STRIP CLUBS, HELL HENCE SEX.

How would we look cryin' over every fuccin' body? I'm tellin' U something about ME at least, I used to be filled with PRIDE but under that was FEAR & TREMBLIN'...

FEAR at not being EXPOSED for my SENSITIVITY and taken for granted &

ALSO FEAR OF ABANDONMENT...

IT caused MANY arguments throughout my LIFE because I DID NOT WANT TO SHOW MY SENSITIVE SIDE TO EVERYONE. I would either storm out in anger, completely ignore someone, or shut down emotionally. It's not healthy but that's how I am. I am tryna change but I do feel like we need some level of PRIDE. IT is caused by GENERATIONAL PAIN. THE PAIN of heartbreak, THE PAIN from racism, THE PAIN from rape, THE PAIN from abandonment, THE PAIN from loss, and THE PAIN. THE DARKNESS THAT ENSUES is unbearable and U WANT TO NUMB THAT PAIN AWAY=PRIDE.

THE STRUGGLE is real and as sensitive as I AM deep INSIDE and INSECURE my PRIDE takes over 4 ME at times & THIS is what I'M working ON...

It's hard to be ONE with someone for many YEARS, and have CHILDREN 2gether and to be filled with PRIDE. I'm tellin' U though, when it comes to goin 2 battle 4 your KIDZ that PRIDE is needed. When it comes to dealin' with INJUSTICE, RACISM anything like that that SHIT is needed. Every RACIAL slur even cuts UR SOUL deep if u LET IT. PRIDE HAS TO COME OUT SOMEWHERE!...

For me, I want to unwind my PRIDE with my King. I want him to do the same. Although, we are similar in that way and stuggle with the same thing. We both had been hurt and don't want to see each other vulnerable. I find it the most hilarious after Lovemakin' when we feel most vulnerable but then we argue the worst afterwards from this vulnerability. It's interesting if you think about it. Pride can actually be a beautiful thing if you get rid of the stigma. It's telling u that you don't really know a person if U still feel a level of their pride in your relationship. It is also sayin' HEY this person is HURTING. If u are EMPATHETIC u wanna know Y. IF and only IF that person let's their guard DOWN that is USUALLY someone worth LOVING and worth YOUR TIME. IF that person is ARROGANT and PRIDEFUL well...I have no words for that. IF someone is HUMBLE and PRIDEFUL U can grow from that. This is actually what I love about my HUSBAND.

> Lately, I been really opening up 2 him.
> It took us 8 years together.
> 3 kids in Heaven.
> 3 kids on Earth.
> NOW we get each other.
> BEFORE we were still learning about each other.
>
> I appreciate our growth.
> I appreciate him.

PRIDE can really delay being close in 1 with someone.

ONCE u reach that UNDERSTANDING it can be a beautiful thing.

(DO. U. LOVE. MY. THORNZ.? DO. U APPRECIATE. MY. ROUGHNESS.? DO. U. UNDERSTAND. MY. EXISTENCE. IS. UR. AIM. 2. PLEASE. MY. KNEEZ. R. ROUGH. FROM. MY. HEART. IS. CALLOUS. I'M. UR. DELIGHT. I'M. UR. SIN. I'M. UR. HEAVY. I'M. UR. KIN. I'M. UR. LOVE. I'M. UR. LIGHT. UR. MY. SIGHT. WALLZ. PRIDE. SAYS. U. AIN'T. I'M. TELLIN'. U. U. LOVE. DEEP. SO. CRY. BABY. BETWEEN. UR. LEGS. BETWEEN. UR. BELIEFS. IF. UR. SPECIAL. 1. SEES. UR. TATTOO. TEARS. IF. THEY. PULL. U. BACK. LET. THEM. STAY. 4. AWHILE. 4 LIFE. LET. LOVE. REPRESENT. WHAT. IT'S. MEANT. 2 REPRESENT. PRIDE. IZ. NECESSARY. PRIDE. CAN. BE. EXTRA. LET. UR. SOUL. IN. IF. U. ARE. ABLE. 2. FEEL. FREEDOM. AT. ALL. ENSLAVEMENT. IZ. REAL. WALLS. WE. CAN'T. AFFORD. 2. LET. DOWN. SKITTLEZ. $20. STRAPPED. TUSKEGEE. PRISON. HOSPITALZ. MALPRACTICE. DISRESPECT. KING. &. QUEEN. UNDERGO. SO. MUCH. STRESS. PRIDE. CAN. BE. TRAUMA. TURNED. INWARD. MY. SOUL. IS. STILL. DARK. WITH. TRAUMA. CHAINS. DECK. IT. OUT. BUT. IT'S. STILL. THERE. SPEND. SPEND. SPEND. IZ. MY. MONEY. HABIT. BUT. PAIN. REMAINS. ON. DECK. I. NEED. 2. SPEND. TIME. LOVIN'. MYSELF. AGAIN. U. FEEL. ME.? BABY. WALK. AWAY. EVEN. IF. IT'S. FOR. 1. SECOND. &. SILENTLY. SHOUT. EVERY. !!!!!!!)

Eight

COUNSEL.

I seeked WISE counsel, that told me that I should tame My SOUL.
OF a CHRISTIAN faith (Or so I thought), that was the right way to go.
It stemmed from BELIEFS but did it STEM 4 NAUGHT?
I wasn't TAUGHT, I RAN, I FOUGHT.
I Thought, but was TOLD not 2 RELY.
DEEP down, I felt WISDOM, DEEP down I CRIED.
WHO could UNDERSTAND? Who COULD FEEL?
WHAT is real 2 them, WHAT IS REAL?

COULD u EVEN recommend SOME1,
THAT won't TAKE ur SORROW 4 lack of FAITH?
COULD U EVEN MEET SOME1,
THAT HEARS U ON A SPIRITUAL PLANE!!!
FRUSTRATION LOOMS...
IT SEEMS I'm INHERENTLY BAD,
& I PROVOKE THE GOOD
AT least I THOUGHT THIS WAY
When MY SEX DRIVE young
PUSHED away MY SISTA
My BEST FRIEND...
OR when MY PAIN,

& LACK OF FORTUNE,
Made OTHERS not FUCK
With ME
DAMN I was 2 MOTHAFUCKIN OPEN.
2 MUCH cussin'
SIGNED the CHURCH.

WHERE can I turn 2?
WHO truly cares?
I FELT my knife against my chest bare.
I FELT my TOMBSTONE KIN.
GRAVE AGONY.
DEATH ANGST.
PAC man u breathed life.
That's the counsel.
That & My HERB.
WRITING LEAVES THIS PLANE.
SINGING UNPACKS.
I'M FORCED 2 STAY.
LIKE LUCY, SUICIDE TEMPTS ME.
COUNSEL TELLS ME NA FIGHT BACK.
COUNSEL TELLS ME NA FIGHT BACK.
ANCESTORS.
ANCESTORS.
SIGNED WITH LOVE.
FROM ANCESTORS.
CANDLES.
INCENSE.
FRANKINCENSE & MYRRH.
CLEAN UR HOUSE.
CLEANSE UR SOUL.

I'M TOO MILITARY WITH MY WAYS.
FUCK IT. PUFFIN' MARYJ.
WHILE BUMPIN' MARYJ.
WATCHIN' NWA.
TODAY NEVA CAME
UNTIL U GOT THROUGH YESTERDAY.
THINK ABOUT IT.
U DON'T NEED TO PAY A COUNSELOR.
TO FILL U WITH SELF DOUBT.
U DON'T NEED UR PAIN AROUSED.
DOUSE THAT SHIT SPIRITUALLY.
IT'S DEAD WEIGHT.
UR ALIVE WEIGHT.
UR LIVELIHOOD IS NECESSARY.
U need 2 be here is what I was told.
U R MEANT 2 BE OLD.
COUNSEL.
COUNSEL.
HUM THAT TUNE.
DANCE.
SING.
WRITE.
STAY CREATIVELY INTUNED.
DO WHAT INSPIRES INSPIRATION WITHIN U.
IF MONEY DIDN'T MATTER>>>

(I. felt. My. soul. Shake. That's. How. u. Know. this. Is. real. I. know. u . question. if . this. New. counselor. Will. get. U. u. Would. Do. anything. to . let. Go. of. That. pain. U. question. Ur. earthly. Existence. Is. it. in . vain.? Counsel. Can. get. U. around. a . fight. or . back. In. What's. True. is. What. will. Heal. u. And. speak. Wisdom.

That's. True. heal. Ur. being. Hear. ur. Heart. Beating. ? That's. The. healing. That. u. Deserve. I. could. Go. on. and . on. Like. most. Counselors. Tend. 2. do . 2. Get. money. From. u. But. na. I'm. going. 2. Say. it. Like. it. Is. meant. To. be. Said. counsel. Is. personal. It. has. 2. Resonate. Within. u. In. solitude. Lightly. Chant. Every.)

Nine

DARKNESS.

"I turned away from DARKNESS, but did it turn away from me?"

Why am I so scared of U Darkness? This weed feels so good.

This chapter is a little much for me. I'm honestly struggling writing it.

I'm not tryna be entirely blunt. I'm tryna leave a level of mystique about myself.

I think we should all live by this law and have a veil over our hearts a bit.

The bible would probably tell U the opposite.

I do remember a passage about a veil though.

I feel so far removed and yet so close 2 God.

With God, I feel this darkness looming at times though, perhaps it's my Mental.

Perhaps it's not.

There's this spirit of Suicide I fight from time to time.

I fight back with Rhyme. I fight back with boxing. I fight back with crying. I fight back with pride.

I fight back since I could fight back.

I fight the spirit of alcohol, but I'm not an Alcoholic.

They go hand in hand. I used to drink when I was very sad "on the edge" I used to say back then...
I wanted something to ease the darkness in my head.
I didn't wanna sleep with strange characters or feel caressed all the time...
Sometimes I just wanted ta puff a black n mild.
Other times, I wanted to listen to some Music.

I wasn't all bad but I wasn't all good.
I did embrace darkness thinking it was light.
I rejected light thinking it was darkness. (chapter; Next—)

I feel a slight block talking about this subject.
Maybe I am just a sore vessel.
Maybe I am just me.

I think I need to just accept my journey. Right now I am having a hard time.
I can be colder than ICE. I can also be sweeter than PIE.
It all depends on my SOUL. whether I feel darkness or light.

Darkness can burn U to ur core. Light wants U 2 be aware of the other.

DO they mend together? Do they vibe?

I'm not sure & neither am I?

IS it real? IS it a battle?

I'm not sure about this either, all I know is what leads to vices.

I think these vices are darkness or as I would like to call it the in between.

It's a gray area to me.

I feel like if it was Darkness it would completely take over being.

IF being is unscathed, is it really darkness to ye?

All this talk in the church about the Devil?

Why when U accept that it is an entity does it seem to flee?

I say it because I believe the devil, if there is one, is a spirit.

I believe u create the devil in your mind.

I believe racism is the devil.

I believe hatred is the devil.

This may just be nicknamed Evil.

Evil is an easier term on my brain.

There's something about going to the church and talking about the devil,

That sends panic down ur spine.

When u wake up from a couple of near deaths or at least unconsciousness,

U C things a lot differently.

I believe God can reach U anywhere.

I believe Darkness does coincide with light.

Balance is what I C and believe 2 be true.

Unless U go through life Innocent & Unscathed.

It's very hard 2 not have anything U struggle 4.
Spirit is meant 2 connect and soar
We long for the SORE to be mended.
Hence U may search 4 darkness
U may fall to darkness.
U may worship darkness.
Ur broken most likely.
Maybe U believe yourself to be inherently bad.
Because you've fallen on bad, been told that, or just are.

I fight my Vices, maybe U embrace URz.
Whateva U wanna call them.
Darkness, Demons, Vices. (DDV)

(AM. I. AN. ACCOMPLICE. 2. DARKNESS. OR. DO. I. WALK. IN. LIGHT.? I. GUESS. MY. PATH. IS. NOT. DEPENDENT. ON. ME. I. FALL. OVER. THEN. I. BOUNCE. BACK. BY. GOD. OR. NOT. MY. OWN. STRENGTH. OR. NOT. SHOULD. I. ACT. LIKE. I. AIN'T. SEEN. SOME. SHIT. SHOULD. I. ACT. LIKE. THERE. IS. ONLY. GOOD.? SHOULD. I. IGNORE. EVIL. OR. PRAY. IT. AWAY. FUNNY. WHEN. I. WITNESSED. SO. MUCH. EVIL. &. PRAY. NOT. 2. IT. JUST. KEEPS. ROBBIN'. MY. JOY. BUT. THROUGH. THIS. EVIL. U. GAIN. PERSPECTIVE. EITHER. IT. OVERTAKES. U. OR. BY. CHANCE. GOD. PULLS. U. THROUGH. I. DON'T. BELIEVE. FOR. ONE. SECOND. GOD. WAS. ABSENT. I. BELIEVE. IN. TRIALS. &. TRIBULATIONS. UR. BREATHIN. EVERY. (LISTENIN' 2 HELL 4 A HUSTLA—2Pac))

Ten

LIGHT.

I don't know where I am going all I know is my SOUL desires light.
Am I good enough to make it into Heaven?
Are any of us Inherently Good?
Is there Good laced with Evil?
Is Myrrh laced with Liquor?

I don't know if Light is what we think light is.
Although I do believe AfterEarth is peaceful, I believe it is also a bit final.
Light needs connection or it dies. I believe that is why people tend to fall to darkness.
Let's focus on light.

I C the light in UR EYES.
I C the light in UR LAUGHTER.
I C the light in UR PERSON.
I C the light in UR WALK.
I hear GOD in UR TALK.

I feel presence.
I feel movement in my soul.
I hear song.

Light doesn't leave U it embraces U.

When I had those near deaths, the first experience wasn't the best.
That is when I believe I was at my worst down a bad path.
The rest, I was covered on every end with LIGHT.
I woke up craving AFTEREARTH 2 be with the creator of LIGHT & ___.
I left that blank in case U don't believe God didn't also create darkness.

U ever been in the midst of darkness & all U feel is light?
I've been here 2.
I remember feelin' Crossed.
A term meaning my spirit felt crossed.
Once this happens U start strugglin, spiralin.
Once U C and experience a different level of evil.'
U cry out 4 light.
U cry out 4 light.
U cry out 4 light.

Is my time here in vain?
Is my time here 4 naught?
How do I seek something?
I wasn't taught 2 seek?
How do I embrace something?
When I wasn't taught 2 embrace?
I was taught 2 brace 4 panic.
2 go to sleep sore.
2 be at the cusp of death so many damn times.
All U desire is PEACE.

When u smoke 4 clarity.
When u caress that bottle.
When U do what U do.
When U Do wAt U Do.

(This. chapter. Is. shorter. but . the. Thoughts. Stay. long. in . my. Mind. i'm. At. a. Point. Where. Light. even . is. not . all. Light. Am. i. AGT.? I. think. So. I. also. Think. Not. I. used. 2. Try. to. Fight. What. was. labeled . as. Intrusive. Thoughts. Until. i . accepted. That. they. also . exist. Light. Is. easier. 2. meditate . on. It. helps. 2. Cleanse. Ur. heart. And. soul. Each. night. I. remember. Listening. 2. D'Angelo. Just. starin. at . my. Fan. or. Nights. Where. I. would. Listen. To. feel. It. in. the. Air. on. Repeat. Nights. Where. I. would. Listen. Were. the. best . nights. There. Would. Be. times. I. would. Not. hear. For. months. On. repeat. There's. Something. About. When. U. go. Numb. that. makes . light. Flee. Light. Is. still. There. But. silent. Is. that. Light. Candles. Romance. Laughter. Love. This. is. Life. walking. In. Light. But. Not. everyone's. Light. This. is. Light's. Portrayal. When. U. Feel. light's. Betrayal. &. U. lose. Light's grasp. it . is. Hard. 2. Come. back. 2. But. u. Grow. 2. A. deeper. Appreciation. EVERY.)

Eleven

VENTING.

As tearZ rush to my eyes,
I feel as if I'm a vessel but is it a vessel of love or a vessel of pain?
I feel tight in my chest.
I feel hurt by this country.
I feel hurt in my family.
I walk around with scars emotionally.
Who truly gets me, is what I've asked my whole life.
I don't know who to turn to.
I don't know who can actually bare my heartache.
I don't know why after all this time I didn't go numb.

Why do I always take comfort in dead artists?
Why do I seem to neglect the life within me?
Why was I drawn to negativity for so many years?
Funny thing is now I just desire peace.
I've went through such a journey spiritually.

It's a journey being a mixed woman.
When there is no one with your exact mixture.
Not only that but society tries to dictate what U R.
Based on what U look like but not exactly what U R.
I've experienced racism, I've went through a journey
With how I identify.

I used to Identify as an Arab, until I realized Egyptians/Palestinians are not.
We are African by DNA but take on the Arab language, linguistics there is so much 2 it.
This country honestly doesn't want us to feel whole.
The minute they clumped us all together.

We have Racial trauma.
Imagine being watched.
Y do they separate us again?
What R they afraid of?
Y do they hate Muslims?
Y do they clump every "Arab" as an Muslim.
Y do they clump every "North or East African" as Arab.
This country is backwards.
This country is Obsessive with
Wanting 2 classify U.
Nosey & busy-bodied.

This country wants to be racially inclusive.
But be racially divisive at the same exact time.
It's the little triggers that make the gun smoke.
IF u get my reference.
It's having 2 think like this in whatever U do.
Then 2 be labeled as paranoid.
Ha. I laugh at that label.
Spirituality bothers this country.

We should all just work a 9 to 5 right?
Or 12 hour shifts?
Or multiple jobs 2 make ends meet?

Right?
We should all be Robotic.
No feeling. No Pride. No Emotion.
WE should ALL wave an EMPTY flag.
(if it makes U comfortable WHITE america so be it).

Whew...

I feel so conflicted in my heart.
Having a part of me that is white.
I hate a part of myself.
The other part of me is oppressed.
This constant fucking war.
This constant fucking battle of being mixed.

Can U Relate?
Look AT me without UR privilege (If UR White...)
Innerstand my Perspective of Pain...

Colorism Stings.
It angers UR being.
So does racism.
So does being told because U are light skinned.
U will get treated better when white people know
U R NOT one of them...
When everyone knows.
U R Not one of them...
It's painful.
ScarZ.
Underneath there is fear.
Of being alone.

OF being misunderstood.
OF being feared for how U look.
OF being killed.
It doesn't matter if U R mixed with white.
Society doesn't see that no matter how light.
Just know that U have to learn to love yourself.
It usually happens after U lose yourself.
I get memories of multiple past lives.
IT leaves me bitter, angry, and confused.
It could be healing in time possibly.

2 Be Continued (PT. 1 of 2)

(Time. could. Possibly. Add. salt. 2. Ur. already. Wounded. Soul. or. Heal. it. if . u. Believe. in . earthly. Healing. If. u. Believe. There. is . a. positive . stance. to. Take. from. Each. dagger. To. ur. Heart. And spirit. U. have. 2. give . a. Partial. Fuck. I'm. seeing. U. have. 2. Have. pride. And. humility. Simultaneously. My. heart. Is. bleeding. In. this. Chapter. Since. The. chapter. On. darkness. I. felt. Spirit. Move. I. knocked. Out. 5. Tracks. In. the. Studio. I'm. at. a . vulnerable. State. Of. being. That. I. can't. Puff. away. That. meditation. And. prayer. cannot . help. I. get. Like. this. when . I. want. 2. Vent. There. Is. no. one. Alive. That. can. Relate. At. times. I. am. a . soldier. But. at. Times. The. tears. Burn. my. Eyes. I. have. Scars. There. 2. My. deepset. Eyes. My. Deep. Set. Eyes. Looking. Back. on. What. I. went. Through. How. I. was. Shouted. Every. While. Unconscious. At. my. Lowest. Point. Being. My. Own. Advocate. I'm. Glad. I. made. it . through. Trust. In. One. Love. 4. One. Love. Trusts. In. U. EVERY.)

OUTRO

I need somewhere to vent my thoughts...

I feel like I don't fit in anywhere being mixed. On top of being mixed, I am Egyptian/Palestinian/Italian. So Basically, Black/Latin (White)/ & Afro Asiatic.

I'm Invisible. We are seen half the time as Puerto-Rican when we're mixed, then we say what we are & we watch our friends disappear...

Am I Arab? Am I Middle Eastern? Am I Black? Am I White?

I was called a Nigg**.
Told this wasn't my country.
Microaggressions.
Racist first Impressions.

What is there 2 Embrace?
My Mixed face?
My light complexion?
My brown freckles of my once brown skin?

My 7 tattoos?
My Sexiness?
I mean my husband is fond of me...
He loves how my curves hug him.

OUTRO

& Yet I still feel "Off".
I never know what label I'm getting slapped with being mixed.

I have to tell myself that I'm beautiful.
I hear my Ancestors speak to me.

Calling me "Habibti, Amour".

I miss my Grandmom, "Tata". <3

I feel Insecure being Mixed especially with Age & Kids & My Hair,
that is now starting to get thinner.
So much of my Pride was in my Hair.
Now What?
Slick it down and focus on my edges?
Or cut it all off? Choices.

I learned to embrace my thickness.
Can I also embrace my thinning hair?
I'm afraid on this journey.

Can anyone relate?

Is it a Mixed Girl Thang?

Fuck it. My Afro says Middle Eastern is a Phony label.
It's not as big but still present.

R U STILL DOWN??

OUTRO

Fuck an outer conflict, have you ever felt a conflict within?
Like Bloods vs. Crips?
Latin Kings vs. MS-13?

What side are you permitted to choose?
When everyone sees a different side of you?
Who are you?
Racial Trauma...
I-N-V-I-S-I-B-L-E...***

Do you think this is a joke?
I can't check off X
Or Y
Or Z.

Without pissing off a side.

Then there's the issue of not fitting in racially anywhere?
Who are my people?

My people turn away from me.

I keep running back only to be hurt.
I scream I ain't white to other POC. but hear that white voice come out,
from all of those customer service jobs.

Am I racially Ambiguous? I think so...

Exotic isn't so fun.

OUTRO

I'd rather claim one.
Sex is the only time I don't think about this.
I can lose myself.

Someone bridge this painful gap. (Maybe it's me that needs to).

This ain't my soil.
This ain't my language.
What is my Native tongue?

I'm light. My DNA Black/Asiatic +Northern/Southern Italian & White.

Half & Half.

That's why I'm light.

That's why my freckles are Brown.
My hair, Black.

I don't look one way.

Exotic is a bird to me.
A Petting Zoo.

I, I, Long 2 Be Free...

What does Freedom look like?

Is it an impossible concept we long 4? Is it financial, spiritual, out of this world?

When can we stop being afraid?
"Exotic" Women have fear.
Of getting hurt by the Cops, Medical professionals, the list seems short but it doesn't stop.

We don't know how you see us.
Let me repeat.
We don't know how you see us.
I think you get the point.

Am I more free being mixed?
I say No. U may disagree.

I'll explain why.
Just listen.
Hear me out.

Being Exotic, or Mixed can go a couple of different ways. 1.) You're insulted and someone either doesn't know how to label you racially and it turns into aggression or 2.) They assume what you are. I'm come across 3.) (The most frequently) Racial Microaggressions.

"Oh, You can't afford that."
"Do you want me to put this back? x3"

3.) May seem "Harmless" to the offender but it is not to the "Receiver".

OUTRO

The trauma from it feels the same. Angry, hurt, belittled. Sometimes embarrassed. It's more subtle so you can't always point it out. #3 is what I experience the most being mixed.

Race got us all fucked up in the head, walking around with trauma wounds.

I used to think I was a straight up White Girl. Society told me No. I started hearing Exotic, Mixed, Spanish, Black & White.

It would bring me to tears at times not fitting in nowhere, and when you're light-skinned and mixed people tend to deny your experience.

When I was 5 years old I went through my 1st racial trauma. They forced people of color on the back of the bus. I took a stand and took this white girl's seat (we didn't have assigned seats) would you know, I was yelled at and humiliated while the bus driver told me to move, she would not even drive the bus, she sat there yelling at me to move, and by this time I was crying. I knew something wasn't right. I didn't move. Not many times did my mom have my back with stuff like that, but never again did I ride that bus again after that. **I didn't know about Rosa Parks...I just wanted that front seat...**

Alexia Zakariya has been writing since she was inspired in High School by teachers she had there that put the spark in her for her writing. Prior to this, she always journaled, but never thought about pursuing publishing her works or taking Honors English classes for writing. She was greatly encouraged in this area, then she was published when she was Eighteen years old by World Poetry Movement.

Then again, when she was 19 years old. She went on to publish another work when she was 22 years old entitled, "Raw and Uncut Poetry" which was unfortunately pulled due to disputes with the publisher, pulled by the publisher. This did not stop her from going forward however, she then published her work "Warmth N GreenZ" which was another poetry book published by Subterranean Blues (Rebecca Anne Banks).

This book is available for purchase. This is her next book she put out which is not a Poetry book per say but written from Poetic lenses. It is published by her & her husband's publishing label, "Seed Royale Publishing". Alexia Zakariya is also a singer and has went on to put out an EP called "AZA" which is a play off of her name Alexia (A) ZA (ZAkariya). She will have much more music to look forward to in the near future. She is also an Artist and some of her work can be seen in her husband's poetry books. One of which is entitled, "PoemZ 4U and YourZ" and "SouL EliXiR: The WritingZ of zO" by Alonzo Gross. She is planning on releasing more books in the near future.

CPSIA information can be obtained
at www.ICGtesting.com
Printed in the USA
BVHW072240020122
625341BV00001B/19